A THOUSAND WORLDS

A THOUSAND WORLDS

THE ART AND PRACTICE OF HAIKU POETRY

John N. Heil

iUniverse, Inc.

New York Lincoln Shanghai

A Thousand Worlds
The Art and Practice of Haiku Poetry

Copyright © 2005, 2007 by John N. Heil

iUniverse books may be ordered through booksellers or by contacting:

iUniverse
2021 Pine Lake Road, Suite 100
Lincoln, NE 68512
www.iuniverse.com
1-800-Authors (1-800-288-4677)

Because of the dynamic nature of the Internet, any Web addresses or links contained in this book may have changed since publication and may no longer be valid.

ISBN: 978-0-595-37471-7 (pbk)
ISBN: 978-0-595-67507-4 (cloth)
ISBN: 978-0-595-81864-8 (ebk)

Printed in the United States of America

to the poet
of any kind
in every heart

ah, lucky beggar
the bright starlight and cool earth
your summer clothing   Kakaku

CONTENTS

PREFACE

This book informs and instructs you about the adventurous, stimulating and enlightening world of Haiku poetry. Its author takes the classical Japanese poem to a new level of appreciation for English speaking people in modern times.

You will find that an awareness of the Haiku experience leads to an awareness of life itself. Its method enables us to relate more meaningfully to the natural world, while also realizing our own humanness on a deeper level. In the keenness of these perceptions, the Haiku phenomenon can speak about all existence, increase our sensitivity to all reality.

So pristine an art form also has great appeal because it is both simple and subtle, delighting on either basis. Whether writing or reading Haiku—getting out into nature or indulging vicariously in our living rooms—it will prove for many a personal revelation and thoroughly enriching involvement. Get set for what could become one of the most rewarding pastimes of your life; most beneficial, of course, in terms of mental and emotional satisfaction.

THE HAIKU EXPERIENCE

wild geese returning
what draws them calling, calling
all the dark night long   Roka

With a focus on nature Haiku is the simplest of poetic forms, one definition being "playful phrases." As such it is aptly described because these concise artistic renderings are a delight to read and write. This introduction considers what the Haiku poem is and how to appreciate it. We also explain the process when composing these brief affirmations of a sensibility all possess who appreciate our world, its natural beauty.

The major part of this book includes 669 of the author's own Haiku poems. They recall what I feel were meaningful reflections on my interaction with nature over many years. Most were recorded faithfully at the time, some in retrospect, and a small number from general knowledge. Readers accompany me to four regions of activity: mountain, desert, ocean, and the forests and lake country of the American Upper Midwest.

The Hokku, Haikai, or Haiku poem as it was finally identified, evolved from at least a millennium of Japanese verse creations. Its present form dates from the 17th century, having developed specifically as the 3-line first verse of a 5-line Tanka. The Tanka was often composed by two persons as an amusing parlor game, witty exchange, or light mental exercise. Group participation and contests were organized around this popular activity, including longer versions of such poetizing.

That two person linked-verse became something of a cultural happening in Japan, a social diversion referred to as Renga. Due to its prominence in the format, there was an increasing emphasis on that key initial 3-line Haiku component of the Tanka. Eventually it stood on its own as an appealing literary invention, emancipated also from that usually lighthearted endeavor of preceding practices.

Flourishing in the 17th, 18th and 19th centuries with masters like Basho, Buson and Issa, Haiku continues popular today. Indeed, the growth of this casual art form in the past 50 years, especially outside the orient, has been remarkable. For his part, Matsuo Basho (1644–1694) is considered by many the greatest proponent and poet of Haiku, an ongoing spiritual guardian of its aesthetic principles.

As one becomes familiar with the method, that apparent simplicity of Haiku is seen as a somewhat deceptive quality. Although each poem is at most only 17 syllables long in English (usually a 5-7-5 structure), the finest Haiku are highly evocative. They suggest much more than appears on the surface in mere descriptive language. It is one of the challenges of these pleasing offerings. An appreciative reader must use imagination to complete the impression, all that is inferred by the lively content in but three lines of verse.

Thus we could say the Haiku poem is simple to a point. Then that imaginative complement emerges, first, as the poet reflects, and second, as the reader completes his or her own interpretation based on what is presented in the written words. These degrees of meaning can expand indefinitely, while not interfering with that original direct effect of the simple Haiku itself.

As children we were told: "Good things come in small packages." There is a school of thought that suggests whatever is simple in life is wisest and best. The Japanese people have always valued the diminutive. An island nation confined by geography it is a concentrated society, most of its citizens living in relatively small residences on small plots of land due to space restrictions and, in recent times, high property values.

In those densely populated coastal regions the masses have adjusted admirably, Japan having one of the lowest crime rates anywhere. And, it is this adaptive community that holds dear those enclaves of outdoor life and wilderness available on a limited basis, but without much accessibility.

Art imitates life, and the Japanese developed bonsai trees that grow in miniature and form marvelous displays; little ponds of carp or gold-fish, and carefully confined rock gardens, are a paradise of necessity; spare but spectacular wood-block prints and fine silk-screen designs are treasured as a precious legacy; there are small jade carvings and cultured pearls of modest price; hand-painted Nippon pieces, colorful Imari ware, Satsuma figurines, scenic portrayals on ceramics, tiny cups for the tea ceremony, are all fragile tokens of a profound Japanese discernment; and, a culinary art celebrates dainty raw fish entrees (Sushi) that enthuse gourmets internationally. Sumo wrestling, one of the oldest of Japan's martial arts, utilizes a restricted sacred circle only 4.55 meters wide to conduct those brief athletic encounters. And, most recently, efficient, compact consumer electronics products, and down-sized cars popular the world over, are Japanese made.

The disciplined, discriminating, unified and pragmatic features of a national character fit well with the concept of Haiku. An understated and cannily compressed fidelity to life as it is, is indicative of these poems that incorporate their own kind of compelling minimalism. The Japanese developed the unpretentious Haiku which, while virtually ignored by Western scholars in the past, is now something of a signpost for the revival of an interest in poetry generally. The novice aesthete can learn from it and grow accordingly, what in modern times and a sophisticated age is an ironic testament to this value of the truly artistic in any form or timeless dimension.

When Haiku is compared to different types of this emotional and rhythmical language of the poet, avoidance of the excessive and egocentric reveals a certain genuineness of its inspiration. Nobody impugns one of the arts or integrity of unconventional contemporary styles, which also indicate a spiritual source as in the "Source" of all life. However, the simplicity of whatever mode with its crisp, economical and cohesive dynamic, has a lot going for it. That greatest of all poets William Shakespeare said: "Brevity is the soul of wit." Haiku obliges magnificently, as well as being far more than the common versifier's usual, that is to say ever so simplistic craft.

> this immense sadness
> after all the bright fireworks,
> but look, falling stars   Shiki

In addition to its uniform 17-syllable framework, there are three principal characteristics of the Haiku poem we will elaborate on. These are: sensitivity to nature; that degree of suggestibility already referred to; and, what is the essence of Haiku, a relationship between two dissimilar ideas or elements, one being the subject matter in nature, the other a human response to it. This third attribute is the poetic inspiration itself, that mysterious leap of imagination akin to all artistic endeavors.

Preceding this analysis there are several noteworthy considerations regarding our main theme. A good deal of sentiment is expressed in Haiku as in all poetry. These feelings of poets are an important factor reflecting the deepest intuitions of one's humanity. The poetic impulse, then, is best characterized as a freedom of feeling that accounts for its plentiful endowment.

Furthermore, Haiku's message is never philosophical, that is, any search for ultimate truths. These verses are not logical assertions making a case for anything. Nevertheless, the poet's beliefs and ideals are quite apparent, absent any opinionated or didactic conclusions.

That symmetrical 5-7-5 syllable form of Haiku was used for the purpose of enhancing pace and rhythm, when a properly worded verse. The 17-syllable length was established as the approximate time it takes for one normal human breath, inhaling and exhaling. It was also a span long enough to capture that single unified impression of a Haiku poem, as first conveyed to the reader.

There is a generous poetic license in the method of Haiku, more so than for most other kinds of poetry. Words or punctuation are frequently omitted, there may be ungrammatical usage or weak syntax, and contractions are permissible, all due to the spontaneous nature of Haiku and the format's brevity. It is our choice whether with or without rhyme, but seldom are these verses rhymed; upper-case, lower-case, it makes no difference even for proper nouns.

Certain latitude is also granted in terms of whichever subject matter outside nature. This practice has a name, Senryu, which is a comparable form of Haiku concerned with human nature, life situations, and peoples' everyday circumstances. These verses often refer to superficial matters, interpersonal relationships, and may be without spiritual depth or any general appeal whatsoever. All of this is acceptable, yet another kind of Haiku satisfaction albeit a restricted one in some respects.

Our own intentions justify any such variance from the usual standard, in that spirit of Haiku's inviting, accommodative and generous expression. In our present day, a broadening of the Haiku concept beyond the natural world to include just about any observation, or a fascination with the essentially private, is done effectively and entertainingly. If appreciated by the writer and reader, these transitional or experimental types of Haiku—differing approaches suited to the modern mentality—are entirely legitimate.

Indeed, new ways of thinking, expressing ourselves and rationalizing experience by means of Haiku, liberate us. It is to communicate our innermost thoughts and feelings while also sharing with others. Additionally, catharsis for the poet is an important consideration, however achieved. Hence, this optimum utilization of an art form; and, those venerable masters of old would likely concur: what permits of creativity or personal fulfillment is a good thing in any case.

Writing Haiku in English according to these new styles does present challenges as well as opportunities, not the least of which is a divergence from its original form. This might include a variety of free verse structures, including single line poems, and, sometimes, even one word contributions that suggest little more than Mr. Webster's definition. Again, the highly individualized or independent viewpoint comes into play here. It is all good fun and more power to the poet of any kind.

Irrespective of our understanding or openness in this regard, and because we seek artistic merit as an ultimate goal, the aesthetic consideration remains our touchstone. This attraction of the traditional, with its emphasis on a nearness to nature, is for us the real fulfillment and lasting allure of Haiku.

At their best, these poems are a wondrous or touching or nostalgic or comforting or hopeful or joyful or sad or surprising or ironic or splendidly humorous realization of all that is true for us. Moreover, consistently fine Haiku draw that critical connection between the self—one's humanness—and the natural world with which a person comes into intimate contact.

Lastly, we note that some of the original Japanese verses require a metaphysical interpretation because of an association with one of the more obscure branches of Buddhism in that country. In some ways Haiku was a cultural derivative of the Buddhist faith. A respect for life in all its forms and stages is one of its values that likely influenced the sense and subject matter of Haiku originally. Considered philosophically, Zen self-discipline acknowledges a oneness of all life as its accustomed response, as does a principal rationale of Haiku.

> the seed of all song
> in the farmer's simple chant
> while planting his rice   Basho

We consider now what classical Haiku consists of, its fundamental being and poetic distinction. The first of three major characteristics of Haiku, sensitivity to nature, reveals the poet's reverence for so intriguing a world set before us by God. The thrill of this art's inspiration derives from an immersion into, and contemplation of, that glorious realm we come to know so well. One nurtures a love for nature, its many and intricate subjects and processes. We can think of Haiku poetry as a celebration of the universe, when drawn into this transcendent relationship with so astonishing a creation.

To begin with, we must become aware of this kingdom all around us, sensible of it. There are so many identifiable facets of nature to which a person can relate, a thousand worlds we might enter. One is moved by it all, in awe, impressed by this range and variety of life. It is an astuteness developed by all who care to see, a child's gladness on this most elemental level of existence.

It is not surprising, then, that the technique for composing Haiku is learned by letting nature direct us. She is our teacher. This poetic urge originates from an object, event or situation observed in that natural setting. There is an identification of some phenomenon that generates a meaningful human response to it. Haiku's creative power is dependent on just such an objective identity precisely affirmed. The best way to achieve this is by focusing, in a somewhat passive way, on an aspect of nature that gains for us a first impression from which the creative insight develops.

One becomes conversant in the language of this other world, studying it in the sense of being more attentive and knowledgeable persons. We accomplish this by getting out into that environment, in deliberate ways becoming conscious of natural occurrences. To augment our perceptivity, note-taking is in order when seeing something interesting or worthwhile. This first inquisitive venture will at least establish a feel for Haiku. As we so involve in whichever ambiance or habitat, a harmony between all of life and one's own self is ever more palpable. Then, in the Haiku moment, that inner spirit of the natural entity becomes one with our own existence.

This orientation to nature is like that of the creative photographer who instantaneously captures a fleeting impression. Having become curious persons we likewise are observant, with a careful eye for life around us, its many revelations. It is to cultivate receptivity, always anticipating the next promising occasion. And though it would pass, quickly fly away, we hold on to that spontaneous reality. Each poem gives an account of these exquisite images and intuitions afforded us. So, first we are open to experiencing the many attributes of nature; then we respect, honor and record that vision of utmost clarity upon which we have centered.

Nature is a universal language with signs, symbols and recognizable tales everywhere. Whether in grove or meadow or mountain pass, by innumerable means we might receive a finest lesson, determine a greater meaning of life, and find wisdom. Each of our senses can so anticipate this world about us and, as Alexander Pope said: "All nature is but art, unknown to thee."

Some reference to one of the four seasons—tapping into their many moods—is a prominent feature of Haiku and for good reason. The seasons, like the stages of life, play an important role inspiring the poetic imagination. Here is the profoundly sentimental theme, the passing of our days seen with some melancholy but also in uplifting ways. Whereas nature itself commands our keenest interest in this genre, a seasonal perspective definitely complements the Haiku engagement.

This might include only an oblique reference to the seasons, for example, "budding places," "balmy darkness," "weary fields," or "barren woods." But some such recognition is proper, as an intimation of the transient lends its special effect. Still, one need not be too concerned about this; there is an awful lot that can signify summer.

And so, we stand humble before this expanse all about us. The Haiku poem bespeaks a lack of pretense, the commonplace, naiveté and innocence itself. Here is a meeting with natural forces in that peaceable, approachable domain. Because nature, even in its fury and in the trail of the storm is a tranquil phenomenon, so are the Haiku that embody and speak from it. We have wakened to a gracious universe, now sensing one memorable instant and extracting the meaning it holds for us. The ephemeral has passed but we recognized reality in this rewarding way, just then a complete, perfect understanding and privileged view of existence.

"Take time to smell the roses," is a choice bit of conventional wisdom that gets us into the spirit for discerning such basic but resplendent profiles of life. In the great outdoors we have a heightened awareness now, with no interference from our petty or usual concerns. One is able to patiently reflect, as never before gaining an acquaintance with all that is alive. Walking with nature as companion she becomes our confidant at last. Then have we sensed, as Wordsworth did, "her breezes stirring in the soul."

There is a vibrant, ravishing wilderness out there, small segments of it probably not far from where we live. Perhaps the moving perception is just outside our window now. But we need that impressionability of a child to grasp its significance. Nobody says: "Yes, I will now sit down and compose a Haiku poem." What one does is enter nature and effortlessly receive her felicities. Or, maybe a person vividly recalls when previously entering those green, wooded or wind-swept spheres. Taking care, discovering, rejoicing in that well-appointed world, such is the call of a Haiku experience.

And, therein is our susceptibility to the refinements of all nature, the great and small of it. This is what must be fondled, caressed, held gently and with much affection by the poets of Haiku.

> the warm and bright fields
> a monk quickly glances out
> the great temple gate   Issa

The quality of suggestion is a second main ingredient of the Haiku poem. It plays an essential role because of this art's dimensional limits which necessitate the succinct expression. For a poet, the suggestiveness of one's lines is a learned facility that comes with maturity and dedication to his or her art. For the reader, that influence of suggestion

11

becomes ever more apparent as these verses are contemplated in relation to one's own experience.

In the fullness of a Haiku reflection, more is there than that isolated "photographic" image or incident in nature. Each portrait is not merely observed, but also stimulates a feeling flowing from the subject matter. The poetic intent has always been subtle, expressive of deeper meanings and emotional responses. Haiku's simply-drawn picture is evocative, it has overtones, an allusiveness, quite ordinary and yet eloquent in its complete exposition. One is able to see simple things and see splendor in them. These deeper insights prompt us and are followed by widening ripples of suggestion.

We set the scene as that of a long imposing flight of two mallard ducks across a picturesque countryside. Such an image suggests certain things to those who relate some personal awareness to this rather common sighting. To others it may not lend itself to a Haiku conception of the real world.

For the poet finding some inspiration in this present development, an association is drawn and by inference an impression of consequence gained. The heightened imagination achieves this as a restrained, somewhat inconclusive and always suggestive response. This emerges in only two lines and twelve syllables, following this opening line which is nothing more than an observation: "two mallards fly far."

Whatever is hinted at there, it can only be determined by a sympathetic bonding to the experience. The very heartbeat of Haiku is this open-ended quality of suggestion called forth from, and echoing within, the self. Each poem first gives us that picture and establishes a frame of mind. This enables one to broaden the perception until such impressions run their course for whoever reflects on the verse.

That enlightened result, an impressionism of words, is the elusive character of Haiku giving life to this artistic enterprise. The connections discovered flow from our own understanding of that natural visage ever so gently and quietly suggested to us. This initial effect also resembles an artist's sketch, the painting of which is completed in one's more absorbed and patient meditation.

To extend this analogy, an impressionist painting emphasizes color, light and a more subtle emotional response, compared to the striking detail and precise feelings represented by traditional works of art. This kind of resourcefulness is utilized in Haiku, when the faint, attenuated and mysterious produce that chain effect of suggestion from a slightest of visual presentations. Though the emotional content is quite apparent in Haiku, it is that indirectness or subtlety of expression which leads to an expanded consciousness and complete satisfaction.

In all fine poetry there is a surface beauty of language, form and meter or rhythm, but something far more appealing behind these exterior features. If it is not the poet's definite realization, then let it be our own. One is reminded of Keats' line: "Heard melodies are sweet, but those unheard are sweeter." Poets and readers of poetry are who write the verses. Herman Melville, remarking about his great American novel Moby Dick, said in effect: Let all readers find in my tale the meaning their own hearts recognize as true.

In a sense, then, every Haiku becomes our own poem for the additional impressions we bring to it. That latent and imprecise telling encourages completeness in important personal ways. The marvel of Haiku poetry is this: much is left unsaid but somehow readily understood. Often its very silences are most telling. Because of all that can be implied, it is a cordial and magnanimous poetic medium. We complement this inspiration when joining the poet in a partnership of souls, a further interpretation pondered from the depths of our own being.

There is one concluding point on this matter of suggestion. The Haiku poem must not be too nuanced or vaguely communicated. It then loses relevance, congeniality, and, therefore, that universality which is the distinguishing attribute of all true art. The poets of Haiku, dwelling on these portrayals in nature, get something meaningful from them; which is to say, what is comprehensible and enriching to rhe rest of us as well.

Certain academics and critics of the classical Japanese poems anticipate too much subtlety, overanalyzing what they perceive in the lines. A few go so far as to superimpose their own beliefs on the morally neutral ground of the poet; or, worse yet, completely misinterpret what a verse means. Our point is this. All good Haiku, whether traditional or avant-garde, must be straightforward enough to be understood and appreciated for exactly what it is.

The great Basho was an honorable man who later in life became a monk. Interestingly, he looked to the person's character as one important indication of a poet's potential and caliber of insights. Basho was also an idealist, a philosopher of Haiku, who tried to uphold the artistic values he encouraged.

As a poet he emphasized the need to write from the "rules of the heart," as opposed to any virtuosity or cleverness of expression. He felt that the strictly rhetorical phrase, a too self-conscious regard, or any adorned language at all, only diminishes the genuineness of Haiku. These poems must be more than colorful descriptions, fine commentary, or the metaphorical allusion. A verse can be profound he believed, while also simple and spare. Poets were only to present us with natural phenomena, the particulars of a situation, the concrete and meaningful experience, but with no precise meaning delineated as such.

According to Basho, the realness of that impression must supersede personal ingenuity, logical conclusions or vain intellectualizing. That excessive ambition of the charming literary verse was to be sacrificed, selflessness in the interest of sincerity and the plain truth of one's poetic vision. He felt the key to excellent Haiku is this natural expression, a personal modesty rather than any verbal skill and articulation. Illusiveness was the ideal, not the well-reasoned and methodical declaration; a purity of feeling and the austere, rather than elegant poetizing.

He set the bar pretty high. Basho himself had written: "If a person composes five real poems in a lifetime that is to be a Haiku poet. One who composes ten such poems is a master." Thus we can say this standard of his might have been, as a practical matter, somewhat unattainable on any consistent basis. But perhaps Basho would have selected this poem as one of his own ten best of a lifetime.

on an empty branch
a bird quietly at rest
in the autumn dusk

This effort does show reserve, real restraint and simplicity though filled with meaning—that product of suggestion. It reveals, does not explain, as the image alone tells us of sadness with the passing of a year, or maybe life itself coming to an end. We the readers of this poem can imagine all that is implied about our own lives as well.

There can be a happy medium between delight, beauty and what is comprehensible on the one hand, and that elusive, vague quality of an ideal Haiku poem on the other. This is a feasible objective. But a verse should not be that subtle and bare bones for all its suggestiveness, if the power and grace, suitable appeal, and possibly truth or understanding is lost in the process. A liveliness or emotional satisfaction is the key. Good literature of any kind moves us, is enjoyable and inspires in some way.

So we are not going to quibble about this, or in any way restrict what is for us a more satisfying resolution when composing our own poems. We need not apologize for these variant styles or special enthusiasms of ours, so long as they are worthwhile and pleasant to read and write. The vitality and pleasure of an inspiration need not be compromised, even if it means compromising to some extent that ultimate Haiku precept.

In honoring the tradition we have addressed this issue of pure authenticity. All poets of Haiku diverge from that ideal on a regular basis, including Basho, and this can be expected given the vast and varied repository generated by its vigorous and winsome tendencies. If one falls short of that exemplar rule, we still remain sympathetic to the poet. It is to recognize the imperfections and inadequacies of every human being, including artists or practitioners in any field. Happily, however, the aesthetic impression justifies itself, making any effort worthwhile.

A Haiku poem must be from the heart, an honest expression recognized as real in the hearts of others as well. This frees it for those multifaceted powers of suggestion and added layers of meaning. Here is a variation on that theme of Basho's stated in a more explicit fashion, which I believe strikes a fine balance.

> at dusk in autumn
> how contented one can be
> but loneliness too   Buson

The third principle or chief characteristic of Haiku, its dissimilar elements or dualism, crystallizes the concept. We now discover the glory of Haiku, the poetic thrust based on what was seen and then suggested by the natural order. What might have seemed nebulous ideas or abstract notions, nature and its impressionability, are now catalysts of a creative response and more exact understanding of reality.

This illumination of what is most true, this revealing of the spirit or impulse coming from the heart, mind and soul, is what we mean by poetic imagination. Such inspirations originate in the so-called unconscious, but what of their actual source?

The beginning of all creativity, all life, is the divine itself. We can only speculate about this, the basis of all creation in the Godhead, but however obscure a genesis these whisperings of imagination are coming from somewhere and in a precipitate manner. The Greeks and Romans explained it as the work of a Muse, the poet's inspiring goddess. We prefer to say this genius, that all possess to some degree, is a gift of God for which the divine can be given complete credit. At least this is the gratitude we sense.

When the composer Mozart was asked how he could write such wonderful music, he shrugged his shoulders and said: "I have no idea;

the melodies just come to me." Genius, the gift, an ethereal source, divine spark, is it not all the same thing? This moment of recognition, spontaneous awareness, efficacious insights at crucial times in a person's life, inspiration itself, one begs the question ad infinitum by claiming in a dumbfounded way: "It simply happens." Let us refer to it as the creative conscience if you will, that essence, that One and mysterious explanation of all truth and goodness.

These two dissimilar components of Haiku, one a condition in nature and the other our reaction to that particular instance, are illustrated in another poem by Basho.

> the morning snowfall
> that black crow I despise so
> oh, he's marvelous

Here the white backdrop of new fallen snow, probably first observed on rising, serves to highlight the coal black body of the crow. It makes what Basho thought an impressive scene of raw beauty, a kind of pristine world just then. Notably, that difference between black and white in the natural setting, can itself be revealing.

The poet then has his epiphany, afforded by that very bird he so dislikes for its brashness and the nuisance it has become when appearing obtrusive and being such an inconvenience at times. Perhaps the bird flapped its huge wings against his rooftop, which disturbed him; maybe it nested too nearby or took menacing dives at a domestic pet. Possibly he felt crows scared the children, and were good for nothing but cluttering up the landscape while arrogantly proclaiming their territorial rights.

Despite all this Basho suddenly realizes that here is a special work of creation, a living, thriving creature trying to survive in the harsh winter weather. Now sleek-looking as ever, this is a natural object he should really not resent at all, but rather admire for its own kind of perfection lived ever so instinctually the best it could as created to be and do.

He overcomes a prejudice here, matures a bit, reconciles an irrational hatred, and sees the world in this entirely different way for the first time. It is an insight to truth and reality, a liberated thought or impression. Basho's change in attitude is nicely capsulated in his poetic exultation and humble human response, "oh, he's marvelous."

He has acquiesced to the beauty of that natural setting and actual attractiveness of the big black bird, in all its stark splendor as it valiantly confronts those chill wintry blasts. Now there is a certain unity with the creature. That difference between black and white also speaks to his dichotomous attitude until then, as much as love and hate are opposites.

From this one effort of the poet we see nature's serviceability, the evocative possibilities of suggestion, and that lively interplay of two dissimilar ideas—again, one being the subject matter in nature, the other a meaningful response to it. A responsive Basho saw something significant in the ordinary, seeing anew, that totality or completeness of his Haiku moment.

Thus we appreciate how the shortest of poems can become the longest, when a fresh impress of nature connects to the spontaneous though thoughtful and lingering reflection. Each Haiku experience is unique, providing an intuition or personal revelation, a clarity of vision. One has drawn a human feeling from the natural world; then, there is that final unveiling of the abundant poetic response.

In summary, by comparison or indirect association, certain circumstances or objects in that wide spectrum of all creation resonate on a human level to establish a unified whole. It can be a thrilling perception, even a stunning recognition for the poet discovering something so wonderful in the commonplace closely, deeply seen.

What may be near in the present but also distant and past, a tension between the temporary and eternal, this place and that, the great and small, possession and deprivation, growth and regression, coming and going, beauty and the blemished, physical matter and the spiritual, realism and the mystical, and however many more sympathies of our human nature, are represented by the most common object or event imaginatively conceived.

Again, the key to creativity is that relationship of at least two different but pertinent ideas, as the poet distills from the real world a penetrating and ever so special response. Such is the quiet convergence of distinct phenomena that shape for us the order and power of Haiku, its transcendent nature and everlasting moment—shape it in a seemingly unconscious way.

We stress that this qualification of two disparate realities conjoined is the most important identity of Haiku poetry. In learning this art of composition, it is beneficial to emulate the high quality of others' verses. Not plagiarizing in any way, but aspiring to excellence while also adapting to the established standards such as determining that interconnectedness of two worlds.

Finally, you will notice that some Haiku poems seem only images of the poet relishing nature. There is no meaningful perception or general interest on which to build an impression. Possibly such verses are idiosyncratic or too sublime an awareness to be understood by others. It is not what the purists want in terms of those potent contrasting ingredients and universal worthiness of Haiku.

Still, we recall the point made previously, when reconciling the new and the old. These somewhat sterile or lifeless lines of only the visual delights of a poet are also acceptable, especially given any larger output by the individual. What pleases the person, and serves one's own purposes for whatever reason, is a tenable practice though of limited potential.

> my fine house burned down
> but now I see much better
> the great rising moon   Masahide

We should now have some understanding of the requirements and informal technique of Haiku. There is a creative intuition, a discovery, and expanded interpretation of nature's specific circumstances. Such is the potency of these short pieces or little art form. Haiku produces an intimacy and intensity of feeling not unlike that poetic sense of the finest longer works. It too is capable of securing sympathy between us humans, while also nurturing our souls.

We have recognized that the vignettes of Haiku are in nature and we have to be natural about it—genuinely beholden to its spontaneous character and far reaches. One becomes sensitized to that dominion, enamored of such a grand kingdom. Each exposure encourages insight to that broader reality of the Haiku experience. We build on this perception in a delicate fashion. And, it is always a human response to the image rendered, the mood established, which is its universal quality.

I will give two illustrations of how this creative process worked in my own case. Impressions of the natural world may germinate over time, and almost all personal insights of any kind ripen with the experience of our lives. The first of these Haiku developed in my youth, the second in middle age. For each rendering, the various elements of the method are evident to some degree as outlined in the text thus far.

> the bark of strange hounds
> now upon the moon the geese
> there is the changing   Heil

As a young person I had a good dose of curiosity, wondering for example just when the seasons came and went. Was it a particular day or hour; were the atmospheric conditions just right, the temperature a certain degree, the winds conspiring in some way. Or was there a sound indicating the knell for a season passing? What specifically ushered in that transformation of nature? For instance as autumn waned, what would signal in an apparent way the first inkling of winter?

In Wisconsin during September and October, the V-shaped columns of Canadian geese high above impressed us as they migrated south. It was a spectacular occurrence, sometimes 150 geese in one wide formation led by some kind of special creature among the many. Though 1000 feet or more above the earth, one could still hear the honking and only marvel at the birds' endurance with their flying range of hundreds of miles from marshland to marshland, when replenishing their energy.

Later on in my twenties, one autumn night I heard what sounded like dogs barking in the distance; but how odd at that hour, I thought. By chance I looked up at a good-sized harvest moon and saw geese silhouetted against that silvery disk in what appeared an almost surreal event. The angle of their flight extended my view perhaps five seconds or so.

Witnessing something that extraordinary, in one overwhelming impression suddenly I realized that at last there it was; the puzzlement of my youth now satisfied. In a symbolic but also most definite way, the season was changing before my eyes by that deliberate act of nature. It was as though a curtain was being drawn, closing upon her finely spotlighted stage. The three aspects or parts of that episode were clearly, easily identified and then described: the sound, the sight, the insight. They came together to give a lasting impression with which I shall likely pacify my old age as a now unforgettable memory recorded in time.

At age 26 I moved to the Western United States, first to California then Nevada, next to Arizona and back again to California over a period of many years. A new stage of nature had been set before me, and I learned once more the wondrous qualities of our always virginal world.

> mystery of time
> still mighty Colorado
> keeper of all dreams   Heil

Standing anywhere in Grand Canyon National Park downstream from Lee's Ferry, the canyon itself stretching 277 miles, is an awesome experience. The1,450 mile long Colorado River winds through the canyon in Northern Arizona. This powerful river current cut its channel through the gorges over millions of years, and still cuts deeper today. The steep-sided canyon walls up to a mile high, and their ever changing coloration, make this one of the seven natural wonders of the world.

On different occasions I have stood and admired such grandeur, privileged also to see the rapid and calm sections of the Colorado itself as framed by those amazing rock formations. There is something mystical and miraculous about this river, its prodigious development over the eons.

Five new American metropolises, Los Angeles, San Diego, Phoenix, Tucson and Las Vegas, with over 30 million people, would not have developed as they did without the Colorado's enormous water and power supplies. What else could have quenched the great thirst of a dynamic West, isolated, parched and deprived of water as it had been? The Colorado seemed to always direct the Native Americans, explorers, pioneers, settlers, adventurers, innovators, and subsequent waves of migration westward. It was that ultimate destination of hope pointed to, everyone's dreams who came west from ancient times on, in the end all their dreams commingled and ever flowing by.

It was another inspired Haiku as all are whether simple or profound, this one composed away from the site and in retrospect. Again, the parts came neatly together as I imagined so mystifying an evolvement of that unique body of water, its strength and still vibrant influence in the American West, the memories or dreams the river certainly holds as represented and still evoked by what we see today and understand or do not understand about progress, geology and the anthropological in that long sweep and secrecy from prehistoric to modern times.

The power of coincidence is our willingness to make something of it, impressed as we are by the peculiarity and partisanship of fate. Indeed, how much of happenstance is but God governing wisely his universe and inspiring us so to whichever purpose? Life is shaped by circumstances, including now our interaction with nature and what this might produce. For example, at first how one must listen to hear birds in the city, intently listen. But then the chorus is clearly there, background music to all our days. For some it can become such a caroling they hear little else, and only because of a chance perception.

> lightly a new moon
> brushes a silver haiku
> on the tips of waves   Kyoshi

When any of us chose this art form as a creative outlet, by composing Haiku the keen insights will come like everything else worthwhile in life: with enough time and application. In this regard the habitual can be a greatest of allies, and one is amazed at its dramatically more productive results.

Haiku also provides a discipline to express oneself in this limited way but still forcefully and effectively. I have always felt that if we cannot state an idea in 25 words or less, chances are we do not understand it ourselves. Poetry generally, and Haiku especially, develop this faculty of concentration and the cogent declaration.

From Ben Franklin to Ernest Hemingway, Americans have been fascinated by writers who utilize a lean, austere style to convey their thoughts. The Emersonean assertion, those hundreds of pithy expressions of Ralph Waldo Emerson, surprise, thrill and inspire all at once. Though not poetized as such, his elevating prose often reads like the purest poetry when that succinct and finely honed.

Emerson's contemporary in the 19th century, naturalist and philosopher Henry David Thoreau, wrote his marvelous Walden Pond in which there is a virtual bonanza of Haiku-like impressions meticulously identified in nature, with equally condensed, refined and humane exposition. Another poet of their time, Walt Whitman, was as enthusiastic about the native and untamed as he was about a plentiful America. That often staccato account in his lyrical Leaves of Grass, was a succession of seminal sensations drawn from the passing rural areas and enterprising people as he traveled the United States.

In the 20th century, the New England poet Robert Frost was also a master of the simple and subtle, with an inclination to ponder the natural world and pastoral life stimulating as it was. Frost was known for his low-key style, the reticence and restraint, while still lucid and vital in what he had to say. His combining the obvious and profound, with that characteristic understatement, is somewhat like the tenor of Haiku. These lines from one of his most admired poems give evidence of this: "The woods are lovely, dark, and deep, But I have promises to keep, And miles to go before I sleep."

A contemporary of Frost's, the poet William Carlos Williams, likewise affirmed that elegance of the economical and commonplace. He could touchingly describe, in the most literal manner, something as ordinary as a rusty old bucket in a barnyard as it slowly filled with rainwater. His poems also suggest a good deal while leaving much unexpressed. Both Frost and Williams could seize the ephemeral image, rendering it memorable and moving though drawn from the homely or mundane. What might either of them have learned from Haiku? Williams, in fact, was familiar with its art.

One does not hastily read a collection of Haiku poems and expect to get anything from it, either emotional satisfaction or an awareness of that world portrayed. In the modern rush of life we frequently feel, and actually experience, so much less than we could. The bombastic or obsessively weird are usually all that grab our attention, certainly if exposed only to the popular culture.

I have never read a Haiku poem without spending at least several minutes reflecting on the impressions engendered, savoring whatever was offered there in the imagery and poetic associations. We learn to understand poetry by reading more of it; and the more thorough this activity the greater these benefits of pleasure and enlightenment.

the chill of nightfall
does anyone suspect these bells
toll our lives away   Issa

A case can be made that everyone needs some poetry in as driven a day as this, given the specialization of our professions and occupational roles. The spiritually starved life emaciates the psyche as hunger depletes the physique. Now in a post aesthetic (the decline of taste), postmodern (its complexity and fantasy), and, sadly, some would say post Judeo-Christian era, the soul must still be nourished.

While no substitute for religious observance, the poetic inspiration can counter to some extent the numbed existence. Gratifying and carefree ventures are as necessary as our serious pursuits, and a balance must be struck. The broadening effect of a Haiku experience is one activity ministering to this requirement. We cultivate an appreciation of the beauties in nature, that proximity to creation and nearness of God. It is his gorgeous world that so fascinates; and these little gems of suggestion endear us further to the greatest truth of all.

We are also an ever more urban-locked people, residing in large cities that actually imprison us because it takes so much time and effort to get away, to completely escape. Everyone restricted this way is encouraged to become familiar with Haiku, either as readers or poets ourselves, in order to reacclimatize to the natural world. Such participation can invigorate us in place, exiled though we are.

There is an art to being yourself, and the haikuist thrives on such openness that challenges all who would be authentic persons. Paradoxically, another effect of haiku is to lose yourself in this contemplation of creation, likewise an emotionally healthy experience. But we must have enthusiasm for the practice in order to gain so much from it. Like the irresistible curiosity and insistence of youths at the feet of travelers, we eagerly inquire of nature and she speaks in amiable and indulgent ways. It is a revitalizing draught of blessedness before one falls back again into the bland and restricting daily routine.

We should point out that in our analysis of Haiku there is no intent to idolize nature with this immersion into its being. Rather, like Saint Francis, we spiritualize and reverence that magnificent design placed at our disposal, not worshipping or idealizing it in some pantheistic misinterpretation of reality.

No less than Aristotle, that most incisive thinker and extoller of the divine, once remarked: "In all things of nature there is something of the marvelous." Might he have been referring also to this larger perception of its many truths, as discerned in our case by the wisdom of Haiku? One would think the Creator glories in our delight at his natural world. A sense of wonder is good for the soul!

Only the here and now is fully realized. With each event in nature we possess what will never be again, except through ever more tenuous recollections. The vanishing years may hold tightly to some memories never letting go, but guideposts of reminiscence are all the more help-ful. Recording meaningful events renews them, in a sense restoring life itself. Just like in feeble old age that flickering light of romance never quite extinguishes, there can be a thriving world of memories in any such vivid account of those glorious interludes past. Haiku can so enthrall the spirit, free the sad and lonely from the weariness of life, with but a few still glowing and earnest reminders of however long ago.

> a trout breaks water
> beneath it on the surface
> the clouds reflected   Onitsura

The way most novels are autobiographical and utterly revealing of their authors though on a subliminal level unrecognized by the writer, poems disclose much about the poet as well. And, if the heart speaks, we must assume it tells the truth as best it can.

After learning about Haiku poetry in my early twenties, for approxi-mately a 15 year period I would note every significant impression when relating to the natural world about me. One begins to see a lot in nature that would otherwise be missed or soon forgotten, and a notebook attests to this. I was always captivated by the wilds and wildlife ways, those moments of instruction as the young person learns about God's creatures and the astonishing universe they populate. Now years later each preserved reflection recalls for me the precise sensation of those earlier episodes and involvements.

Our interaction with nature when still youthful produces a certain tour de force of impressions in the awestruck and naive. One is stunned by her vagaries, the way that primal response "flight or fight" replays itself frequently in our lives. A person only needed to stop and reflect on those many worlds; or, recall not too much later in exact detail whichever new discovery and exciting event growing up. As I got older I became more nostalgic and this is reflected in my later Haiku. I wanted a permanent chronicle of everything that had impressed me about the environment in which I lived, the nature I had known.

I benefited from living a good part of my life in both the Midwest and West, the Great Lakes region, on the Pacific Coast, and for a number of years in both the Mojave and Sonoran deserts. Observing different sides of nature in each locale, these characteristic variations were entirely persuasive to me. The Japanese masters of old were not as fortunate. Their immobility and confinement at that time limited them, and they would not have had the assorted experiences of most modern writers of Haiku.

For example, the 12,400 ft. Mount Fujiyama near Tokyo, like the ubiquitous cherry and plum blossoms or nightingales and cuckoo birds, probably accounted for a disproportionately high number of Haiku because it was such a focal point in nature. That one mountain might have provided as much inspiration for the Japanese originators of Haiku, as Mount Olympus had for the Greek myth-makers. Each profuse panorama spoke in its own way to the heart's longings, each to some extent filled a spiritual need in peoples' lives.

three most pleasant things
moon glow, cherry blossoms, then
I find silent snow   Rippo (his death poem)

Alfred, Lord Tennyson, the 19th century poet laureate of England, penned these lines: "We are ancients of the earth and in the morning of the times." If it is true that thousands of years from now people will look back at our present generations as yet another refuge of antiquity, and if writings from these times do somehow survive, will they recognize this world of which we are now so indispensably a part?

I refer to our natural world. As stewards of creation, sensitivity to nature cannot help but make us concerned about its perpetuation. This is another advantage of these candid experiences of ours, when valuing and respecting all life forms as we find a way of getting closer to them. Every moment of such contemplation is worth it, and so, the practicality of Haiku as well.

In ending this overview, it is my hope that readers gain from the Haiku experience an appreciation of nature as companion, solace as well as sustenance on this pilgrimage of our lives. My wish, also, is that others learn this wonderful Japanese verse form, creating, composing for the sheer joy of it. Then would one likely have an even greater reverence for the fragile, may I say sacred environment gifted to us. And that is something all would hope for.

Art, the arts, the artistic, are broad concepts indeed, but essentially refer to what is beautiful and original as developed through imagination. Using the term generically, art together with religion are the common denominators of all cultures, as though a foreordained necessity of our being.

These diverse impressions of all artistry also reflect a yearning, even a restlessness of the human spirit. As such art can be a sighting of truth, possibly a glimpse of the divine amid the sometime brokenness and barren conditions of existence. In an instant's recognition, really great art captures all the hope and aspiration of our souls, certitude that life is important and meaningful.

At last, then, let us commend poetry itself. For this is the most passionate of all the arts expressive as it is of the intimate self, a poet's utterly revealing sentiments and nakedness of thought. Likewise a spiritual force, we become acquainted with its language in order to relish the flavor, lavishness and ennobling qualities of these distinctive creations in the lyrical vein.

In any philosophy of art, each of its many effects must be accounted for. So where might the spare little Haiku poem fit into so vast a pageantry? That is the challenge, a marvelous expression from something so slight, discovering the tiny pearl in a whole ocean of wonder.

Haiku is, in my estimation, a primer and perfect place to begin savoring this incredible artistic resource of poetry. Each short verse is comprehendible, brief enough to accommodate the least patient person, the youngest heart. And, I might say, it is a good place to end as well. If we compose these pointed indications or little flashes of the sublime in nature with all the importance they hold for us, we can cherish those memories as much as any worn and faded image in a photo album.

Can one thank the Japanese enough for their contribution to this distinguished world of poetry as reflected in the simple Haiku? It is a modest offering but at the same time, I believe, one of the worthiest in all literature. Why would one make this assessment, when the sophisticates are ready to dismiss such an opinion as that of a dreamer caught in the web of personal fancy?

Because simple things can be the best of all when realized, unabashedly, for the glory and promise they hold. Haiku lets each of us common folk become poets, artists, in speaking the way our hearts would care to speak. This is the truly universal, anyone's poignant vision; this is Haiku.

Let the masters speak to us again of the four seasons of their lives.

in my aged years
now these lovely days of spring
bring more tears instead   Issa

this field of flowers
yes, it is all there is now
brave warriors' dreams   Basho

how commendable
the glorious maple leaves
waiting but to die   Shiki

a loud cutting saw
such is poverty's gladness
in winter's deep night   Buson

HAIKU POEMS OF JOHN N. HEIL

Personal Note

Practicing the art of Haiku I had to develop two qualities in particular. The first was restraint in the interest of subtlety or suggestive poetizing. This I know is the basis of enchanting Haiku. But one must also be understood, and the verses moving or enjoyable. Hopefully I achieved this balance often enough. It is a challenge for me as for others, and sometimes my enthusiasm for nature gets in the way of that high standard of elusiveness.

Secondly, I had to become vulnerable, courageous, and take chances in expressing myself—what I actually felt. Despite any self-doubts, and regardless of how unusual or simple-minded my initiative, likely this was the poetic impulse within me—the freedom it longed for. Whatever originality, grace or vitality in my verses, I owe to this need to be who I am.

dare we now follow
this old trail in the forest,
finding wild flowers

birds on breezes south
so real my sense of things past
that died with the years

the day is over
mingling with an Angelus
cowbells follow home

a dog yelps at night
what have the wilds now taught it
the moon hiding so

winter's bare landscape
still, see how spectacular
filled with emptiness

the great albatross
all daring dreams flying far
their home wind and wave

even the ant must quench
that slightest thirst of all
this care of our world

fresh print of bear paws
fear grasps hold the boy's body
what if there are cubs

gulls answer the wind
waves rest with infinite sands
. sea shells remember

over the mountains
hills, valleys, elms and roses
a moth finds a moth

a whole afternoon
in the forest by himself
the strange-minded boy

in the soft moist fields
inexorable springtime
that march of the mice

faint light of the sun
beaming quickly from the moon
to my lover's face

through all the small stars
and universe crawls the worm
this morning's rock path

a bird's melody
now children, cicada sing
summer arias

in winter's deep cold
six sparrows mingle as one
fitting survival

deer learn their stillness
quietly they leap through brush
then that silent stare

fat frog on a pad
no care, we have forgotten
a whole world afloat

a bug crushed beneath
still squirming its bit of life
I must quickly stomp

God once had this thought
to place the pure white lily
midst all creation

a robin's ice tomb
now finally admitted
all of autumn, gone

this obsession earth
a pebble cast by the sun
in fathomless skies

the countless stars
so impossibly distant
but I must sleep now

from this mountain ridge
distantly a long train winds
the toy of my thoughts

alone in the woods
this remoteness from the world
a thought of one's own

saved in a white pail
the softness of rainwater
grandma's silken hair

the pine tree must be
for all our inspiration
haiku of the heart

sits the huge Buddha
playing with the falling leaves
no wonder he smiles

a monk sounds the bell
his one long fervent prayer
for a waking world

joyful mockingbird
but sadly too, in its strain
every yesterday

bits of antlers, hoofs
where the great bucks did battle
all of life's struggle

transfixed by the clouds
and then I am among them
how to hold the spell

the great star dipper
years since I had played with it
holding memories

a kitten's keen eyes
then the jungle in her stride
across the soft rug

two separate worlds
farmer and sailor afar
now the passing ship

a path in the woods
I caught in the spider's web
my reverie lost

this December eve
on the tip of a bare branch
an ornament moon

cosmic lightning storm
somewhere the borealis
pieces of the sun

such futility
a dog leaping for the moon
my own foolish thoughts

a blue jay glares at me
beauty yet such arrogance
nature's second thought

become the small fern
so to speak from its being,
the masters would say

rats, roaches and spiders
those guardians of virtue
slothful housekeeper

windy molds and crispness
October differences
the world through a tear

happy dainty feet
painting their child masterpiece
so smooth the moist sands

one week of lilacs
so extravagantly daubed
allure her June bugs

through the hollow
a thousand sounds of springtime
quicken and carom

upwind the clear chime
just now how delightful bells
other times how sad

precious condor egg
all civilization waits
on nature's verdict

the crickets give way
to frogs and nightingales
before day may come

nature's violence
such is all its survival
for these tranquil days

pour, pour all you rains
and suit the mood of my world
loss, the loss, this loss

those windblown children
running with the autumn leaves
their phantom piper

night bestows darkness
a warm fire and the silence
perfect thoughts of things

great gray boulder
forever anchored in the field
butterfly, snowflake

in a fold of swamp
the fox quietly nestles
hounds now faintly heard

up then down the hills
they ran to exhaustion, and
the death of childhood

in a fisherman's palm
squirm the slick minnow bellies
that tug of the sea

the garden of stars
or pick a moon from an elm
hold the hand of night

a thousand more miles
insects coming tree to tree
one leaf to the next

whole oceans of storms
the flea barely escaping
one perilous drop

to the forest edge
no farther would the child go
his own fairy tale

the blue of iris
uplifts the more these poor words
of morning prayer

March not knowing how
will weeping come, waiting smile
track the red robin

the huge bowed oak tree
now seeming to embrace me
I lean upon it

seasons of childhood
the baby robin would grow
how quickly it grew

in witching madness
rose the moon silvery round
now become love's coin

that proud cat who caught
a cardinal in our yard
was just killed by crows

this new day; no, no
because it has snowed all night
a new world arrived

bright silver trail
fashioned from moonbeams and bled
the heart of a snail

on an island beach
I rest with the universe
alone upon earth

in the dark cocoon
a caterpillar asleep,
dreams of a sun god

symphonies on end
each pine needle its one note
all the earth a song

the last fallen leaves
riot with swirling snowflakes
two worlds combating

this wind from the west
it is not winter's or spring's
an icicle poised

the strong desert winds
and billions of sand bits
beat against an age

what an extinction
canaries caught in wide nets
for tables of kings

bright water lilies
attract the frog and the fly
nature's deep intrigue

canyon cathedrals
boulders in perfect stillness
a hallowed presence

bear and the beehive
it seems in nature's balance
an unfairness now

sounds, shadows, stillness
the swamp holds such fearsome things
my primitive self

your shocking color
I hope you can still endure
New Years day robin

the cicada shells
summer's emptiness at last
these too humid days

in a few mint leaves
the fresh taste of rich spices
this weedy old field

autumn of our lives
hope now here, and truth enlarged
in every tear

the blizzard has passed
crystals are perfectly stacked
in infinite care

these scattered seedlings
that came from the massive elm
I growing older

the sheep in the lane
all that is past lingers there
a timeless wonder

exhilaration
from high ski slope or full sailed
become as the wind

frost wearies the land
his long year now ending
a farmer walks home

the red rose on fire
where did such color come from
a child must ask this

in winter's deadness
lies the very hope of spring
seed beneath the snow

a marvelous moon
even the homeless praise it
this longest of nights

in February
a shrunken rose on the stem
his forsaken love

I turn to see stars
there is the whole universe
over my shoulder

each step through the fog
could become the vast mountain
life daring me so

by this loneliness
is heard in the river's flow
a voice from the past

the countless sea shells
whichever kept by a child
most precious jewel

the waking of spring
between the warm window panes
a fly has revived

lost, cold and hungry
a dog whimpers in light sleep
thoughts of their faces

the sun at daybreak
a canary rejoicing
in its metal cage

a piece of driftwood
soothing as the sea itself
with flowing contours

yes, this first cool breeze
heralds all eternity
we watch day's descent

the oak is creaking
and the winds so relentless
this burden of years

a rose in the sun
so has it grown lush and tall
this child of a star

we can remember
what the plucked daisy had said
happily that June

the more worn by wind
farmers appear as scarecrows
tending their spent fields

beautiful bird
it must be I you carol
with your angel voice

such long silences
a storm is capable of
then the night is war

it is late summer
waiting on the words of love
the moon must not leave

slowly maple flows
attuned to nature's patience,
choice winter vintage

lilacs sadden us
as when summer soon passes
but now time stands still

the wild violets
held tightly for his mother
May is the surprise

a flooded cornfield
the farmhouse is an island
solitary life

the six robin eggs
as glorious to a child
as the whole blue sky

no use to sing bird
a northern wind is blowing
forever autumn

to fish is to dream
not about catching a thing
idyllic June day

a stolen apple
panting, hiding in terror
its succulent juices

the songbirds of spring
an opera by pure chance
tells the heart's own tale

a slightest tremor
wait, no, not yet the great quake
all life's precipice

he climbed the tall spruce
swaying in the winds on high
foolish, wisest child

four times the stone skips
a great plaything that river
of all the children

faint prints in the sand
who of the ancients walked here
time dissolving all

a wolf at midnight
howls defiance to our world
wilderness' own voice

soft cherry blossoms
nor has one ever listened
to hear snowflakes fall

drown in their rhythms
rolling waves and treasure ships
among the sand dreams

the moon then venus
now saturn and jupiter
the crickets on cue

an old sailor's tale
breathe deeply the purest air
hear of seven seas

how wild the blizzard
but each diamond snowflake
carefully preserved

the fireflies gather
their quiet celebration
amidst twinkling stars

a dry river bed
gold dust or Gila monster
desert hopes and fears

steep cliff, wide vista
the sea sprawling before me
this edge of the earth

the bark of strange hounds
now upon the moon the geese
there is the changing

a church in the woods
uplifting spires of tall pine
all that congregate

bow to the broad ocean
daisy blowing in the wind
your face is the sea

haiku in my pond
would its circle extended
reach out to the world

watching the sun slip
into its watery grave
they must have wondered

serene country lane
sunny green and canopied
could lead heavenward

now lost among trees
chasing a white butterfly
the child does not cry

in some hidden cove
the last surge of mighty sea
its resting place now

bright red cardinal
great herald of better times
this cold winter day

the shade of nightfall
a creeping gloom sweeps slowly
past its autumn hour

on a summer breeze
points the visiting monarch
its mountain kingdom

fall mists on the bog
those far places of our past
how faint the voices

only the jasmine
can lift a fluttering moth
to dance round the moon

the dandelion seeds
thousands on a breath of May
mimicking the sun

                    he falls to the ground
                    the hope, joy, and livelihood
                    all it has borne him

an insect's first throb
the sky unburdening itself
spring flies and flows on

                    every dead mouse
                    must then be accounted for
                    in nature's balance

where did it come from
the first robin of springtim
or had it not left

                              pushing his cart home
                              what a world just happened by
                              sun, sea, moon and hills

in and out the clouds
children now playing with it
a tiny toy moon

                              a bird obeying
                              that dictate of all nature
                              oh great song on high

touching the new print
etched by the hoof of a deer
I feel its dark eyes

with a butterfly
children taste the sweet flower
removed from the stem

little wooden bridge
leaning I feel the river's
desire for the sea

scraping against it
the branches speak eerily
of a vacant shack

terrible hunger
that daring of a fruit fly
such modest demands

　　　　the sudden glory
　　　　from dark clouds sunlight streams
　　　　a heavenly glow

the bare maple tree
stark and gray along with March
its beauty within

　　　　it is the same moon
　　　　but one quickly looks away
　　　　for the winter chill

with every hop
the child intends to capture
a robin red breast

chasing the seasons
ten thousand haiku are ours
but a moment's glance

energetic wren
grasping all the sky above
little burst of joy

a distant mountain
reddened by the light of dawn
holds what gift today

ancient arrowhead
a memory of mankind
gleaming in the sun

slight sting of a bee
summer's only price to pay
these glorious days

held in gentle hands
I feel the universe throb
a tiniest bird

whistling in the woods
I am part of the forest
a bird agreeing

above the city
a black and filthy pigeon
quite elegantly

dissecting a leaf
the boy learns more of nature
his own fine classroom

the night to blind men
is a mysterious thing
part cricket, part owl

ever slightly south
they flutter across the lawn
in autumn twilight

mouths widely straining
distantly a worm struggles
April's urgency

hypnotically
the dark canyon slowly fills
a pitcher of moon

however it scorned
the snail eventually
finds its green Eden

the child on that hill
playing gently with springtime
will she remember

the country draws me
like some pilgrim to a shrine
peasant of my past

dawn twitches in sleep
feelings of orneriness
startle the rooster

God-pitched nightingales
set unheard nights to fluting
play to all my cares

suddenly an owl
warning from a moonless perch
it was his forest

suns and daffodils
the first robin's bolder dream
thrust out your red breast

those shouts of sheer joy
how do they carry this far
from the Hoyt Park pool

in twilight splendor
winds and trees cease struggling
our cares laid aside

the clashing colors
of eccentric old autumn
now dance for me leaves

winter burial
perfect cries of mockery
from a field of crow

with all their steeples
cities seem to always pray
birds soar drab heavens

sped through the hollow
mallards glide onto the pond
I hunt with my heart

why the forest sings
birds enjoy their own sweet song
and warn when silent

the kinds of summer
skies full of bright shooting stars
the reign of fat flies

the wolf and his pack
still, we are one with nature
the bobcats playing

this high distant hill
there lie our days beneath us
and places to touch

glutting the new sweet
a bee engrossed in rose depths
knows of summer's end

Indian summer
all that once sweetened July
now mingle in mists

leafless and songless
the winter trees stand calmly
perfectly themselves

exotic pheasant
not knowing of its beauty
nature's modesty

the snow is silent
but what can so change our world
a child's own prayer

that ceaseless ocean
here telling of many things
the stream of my thoughts

all that might have been
a bell tolls for the dead child
hear the birds of spring

more orange blossoms
or deep snow on the mountain
yes, the whole of life

gone the wild horses
how the antelope hide now
in the short grasses

the sunrise again
that fiery resolve of all fates
told by a rooster

a skunk saves itself
on this perfect summer eve
ah, sublime fragrance

cracked and grassy now
filled only with memories
the old wishing well

a desert tortoise
might it remember the sea
this lost prospector

in the stone birdbath
there are only two robins
but all of springtime

slowly does spring come
each blade of grass a counting
birds go branch to branch

merciful winter
new snow purifies the land
a warmth deep within

are the winds warning
if there is a message here
it sounds threatening

all the world now grants
for the whole of its lifetime
this pond to this frog

a first love returns
this miracle of springtime
in my fragrant sleep

the clear desert sky
so far and fast my journey
star to star to star

birds know not to eat
of the pretty red berries
summer paradise

this joy together
and mutual love of spring
sharing the raindrops

one season must end
for another to be born
the bittersweet vine

that sound of crickets
it could as soon be the moon
scaling the long night

the orphanage bell
it must call as mothers would
his morning prayer

so necessary
one leaf in the far valley
part of the beauty

two miles of ocean
at dawn I walk the moist sands
beachcombing ideas

here the winds must shape
and rush as waves over hills
an unseen marvel

the turtle so slow
very awkward and listless
must strike like lightning

from the old garden
he can tell what hour it is
circling sunflower

the skull of a dog
in suddenly ghostly woods
the boys learn of death

see, the ants rebuild
such devastated kingdoms
a deluge a day

watching the eclipse
in the group standing about
we were like lovers

the snow must first fall
on the last struggling flower
ending all autumn

a spider knitting
so the world would very soon
appear shattered dreams

oh the gladnesses
an entire summer of them
rippling and singing

true flower of earth
in the snows or stifling heat
pines richly scented

the city jungle
where cats prowl about warm days
lone bird on a wire

a struggling spring day
greets the soul as no other
hope is a dull green

breezes blow freely
over a choice countryside,
city lights and dreams

only the birds' songs
quietly through the forest
settle on this pond

yes, as the crow flies
an intentness of vision
and reigns sovereign spring

July sets its sun
a moment's canvas of sky
remembrance the thing

in the beginning
that sudden vast universe
each miracle star

gathering riches
pinecones from the forest floor
decorate Christmas

it is the small fish
that lift the heron in flight
new pond to feed in

a tree bleeds its sap
but all the seedlings in place
woodsmen heading home

the oils of the earth
reproducing its beauty
this painted landscape

the whales gliding by
lightly, with the birds above
their migration south

winter impatience
all the harsh year on my sill
that hiss of a log

garlands of summer
strewn before the lowly mice
oh glorious world

a pearl all the sea
had struggled and strained to shape
for Miss Jones' bodice

the honeycomb now
with all of summer's sweetness
in winter's pale light

to the same flower
the dance of a butterfly
the toil of a bee

a stand of tall birch
classical smooth white columns
the thoughts written there

dusk and eventide
set out their first candlelight
so prompt a north star

aerodynamic
aleap of morning belfries
doves pure and panicked

washed up on soft sands
the limb of a mighty oak
other summertimes

Issa, Basho and Buson
still the masters teaching us
from their springtime tombs

the full moon just now
snails, lovers, owls and thieves know
of its helpfulness

an eye delighting
quickly between the two worlds
moon and midnight bloom

one here and one there
soon now the stunning bouquet
of mere violets

such a great distance
and the mountain unyielding
flower at my feet

the true possessor
florist's art, lady's bouquet
satiated flea

in these countless ways
all the green glory of spring
one stem of sweet grass

in mortal combat
the great clashing sides of March
a crystal, a breeze

upon the dead year
of worn wretched December
a white sheet of snow

over Holy Hill
butterflies slowly making
stations of the cross

leaves crushed in my hand
closing one's eyes to inhale
any great forest

the raspberries wait
for June and sunlight and rain
an old woman's hands

a plump little moon
caught high in the spider's web
I relish the night

the dreams of summer
abundantly do they bloom
in a winter place

a twelve-pointed buck
between the lake and the woods
outliving hunters

so determinedly
the fox digs out a muskrat
I must only watch

have mice ever seen
what the moon really looks like
or am I a fool

from darkened waters
all of nature's hauntedness
the cry of a loon

oh rapturous bird
an immortal tune you sing
see, spring's grand return

strangest impression
there by wide lawns, fresh flowers
it is my childhood

see the soft round moon
in a garden of stillness
suckling the stone nymphs

cold and pure water
from warm rocks a spring trickles
the snows well-preserved

in their scattered fields
how precisely the daisies
apportion summer

star burdened heavens
lighting a path to the shed
caving onto thoughts

nature's composure
that plump rabbit so at ease
though the wilds await

after the downpour
are the grasses that greener
or I more joyful

hawks, swallows and swifts
each diving distinctively
for its own supper

an old swimming hole
young lives left far behind here
a dime in the mud

summer weariness
heat and pleasure drain our days
how gently snow falls

a March raindrop
the first one on my window
this great task of spring

beautiful sunlight
piercing the forest's green roof
what a grace it is

how many summers
this bright lit, warm and vital
does the sun still hold

so intently searching
to find a four-leaf clover
the child disappears

a great fattened crow
takes what is left of autumn
then notices me

this summer day
the river can never wait
yet it always waits

he just walked and walked
all through our years of childhood
sad man by the tracks

hundred degree heat
for four months the fierce desert
sidewinders dancing

from winter's cold grasp
from snow yellow crocuses,
what feats of nature

in their flight away
and that emptiness of fields
the heart longs anew

with a meadowlark
sharing the morning dewdrops
a new golden sun

all that way snowflake
then only to disappear
her pretty eyelash

all those years it came
from where had the river come
nature's hiddenness

the wasp is listless
how the Octobers of life
fade in enchantment

cicadas' lament
or are those screams of delight
summer's long coming

an eagle so high
midst clouds it rules in a way
over all the world

from an apple tree
the boy so happy and thrilled
surveys his summer

twilight-still lagoon
the frog too would hold its breath
to mirror a doe

the daring children
who would leap the wide river
wobble stone to stone

on a garden path
my joyful meeting with worms
sunfish in the lake

it is all the twigs
and great squeaks of mice that make
forbidden forests

to stoop for daisies
is to bow before nature
all earth a garden

along with the moon
I run faster and faster
through the bare elm trees

two doves on a perch
yes, the most contented scene
in all of nature

alone the vast sands
this desert silence implores
a prayerful place

the deep-petaled rose
both honeybee and poet
would search for its soul

bracing our spirits
the year's great transformation
each season its song

pretty butterfly
but oh, children chasing it
such perfect beauty

great lawns and gravesites
not all the flowers on earth
could dissuade one tear

lookout, be careful
the bats have all just come now
oh, another night

past the bay window
for the entire length of it
the blur of a bird

four heliotropes
bend their long green stems in chase
in love with the sun

in the dry creek bed
reeds, twigs and little flowers
lean sadly downstream

a field in twilight
I would join the children there
but have forgotten

pansied verandas
roofs of Bougainvillea
house the placid soul

maggots in garbage
rats nesting in dark alleys
nature's poor brethren

the rains are nowhere
except on those distant plains
tears of farmers' wives

a branch on the path
this forest presenting me
my own walking stick

each day's sad twilight
as though learning once again
the shortness of life

tiny yellow bird
serenading the jailer
who stole its forest

this lush summer place
there are a hundred haiku
not beyond the glen

the vast ocean comes
roaring and stretching barely
to a child's sand pail

could they only know
the one sting is a bee's fate
nature's own reasons

the wisdom of time
by countless adaptations
ground moles burrow on

the mirrored children
bent over a river bank
spring's own vanity

struggle in repose
at once the savage conflict
but peaceful landscape

lustrous black beauty
regal raven who are you
just the same old crow

hidden somewhere far
a trout stream one's very own
the soul dreams of this

a bird's dilemma
fly to feed or rest some more
not just sitting there

summer afternoons
this quiet joy of our hearts
in the slightest thing

the world's building blocks
a single grain of pure sand
one drop of water

                              to reward the birds
                              he planted mulberry trees
                              all their grace and song

winds rustling, stirring
the endless hymn of summer
buzzing, chirping on

                              flowers of the night
                              persisting in loveliness
                              scent my sweet dreaming

on a sunset sea
two worlds becoming as one
glorious embrace

death's hidden places
all nature's secretiveness
where can it be found

who could inhale it
in one rose so much fragrance
maybe all of us

silhouette of sound
stretching into its midnight
a coyote moon

the horns of a snail
then how many slight wriggles
through the morning dew

mountains immense, stately
nature's own self-assurance
now dares the red fox

they call, call again,
now whistling the same fine tune
I answer the birds

creation anew
as though showing gratitude
we search out springtime

a boulder is crushed
eons of gentle raindrops
her patient powers

quickly nine ducklings
not knowing of my revere
paddle behind her

countless are the sands
this desert infinity
of endless summer

plums from the blue sky
a child's summer dalliance
leaping for the sun

the reticent sands
civilizations come, go
that silence again

snow yet summer heat
Fujiyama cools me off
distant, hopeful dreams

city of my birth
stockyards, hops, and chocolate
ah, spring's gentle breeze

the winds remarking
so pristine and picturesque,
I now first noticed

this pond is the moon
the moon has become this pond
night embracing all

the moan of a ghost
or sound of the wilds at night
in and out my dream

in morning coolness
a sunrise paints pheasant wings
completing my day

softening twilight
lends one side of the flower
a new reddish hue

the brook and the bird
nature's most sublime duet
I am being called

the birds' endless flight
there is freedom in nature
and wings on my thoughts

honeysuckle breaths
that full sweet scent of the South
a world all its own

the long dark road home
so many small, silent suns
how keen a deafness

farmers circling fields
their ploughs plodding past springtime
that clock of the land

in webs of midnight
spiders race across the moon
the reach of a thought

all eagles and hawks
diving, whooshing and soaring
nature's fiercest face

what is this presence
the dark night is not alone
oh, that one-eyed moon

a largest black bear
suddenly it disappears
the spirit forest

a frog croaking on
I mimic that dull gruff call
it answers me "no!"

autumn's saddest song
the coo of a morning dove
seeming so distant

sea, land and shoreline
a meeting place of two worlds
thoughts of final things

twigs, mounds, blades and stems
that jungle of the grasses
do I see my world

in eons of time
why would sparrows change the least
such perfect creatures

that awesome balance
between all glory and ruin
little bird please live

tulip-painted yard
from the palette of springtime
spadework artistry

all the cold winter
tending that one violet
how tenuous life

among butterflies
dizzy laughter till tears stream
to ride on their wings

autumn of my days
crescent moon of memories
you hold too many

nature's hiding place
this waterfall in the woods
somehow I found it

pale green hills and vales
just now rising from the dead
miraculous spring

slowly, secretly
wade to the rock and turtle
then its perfect dive

sun marches with snail
up a barren black landscape
sting the rooster's eye

the wholly blank face
of a demented old man
stares at falling snow

all the sky above
commending freedom to hearts
robin's broken shell

pieces of driftwood
in the sea's quiet places
are smoothed for shores

they are here somewhere
mountains, cliffs, rocks and ravines
ancestral spirits

staring at raindrops
the children cannot welcome spring
how slow their year goes

a forest speaking
listen to the thousand sounds
of blindmens' delight

amazing snowflake
each its own perfect design
divinely reckoned

now which to observe
setting sun or rising moon
nighthawks to and fro

with midnight's last sigh
to whom does the moon belong
crickets deciding

the sun seeking out
each smallest insect, all weeds
so lavish its light

we can sense it now
the first fresh air of springtime
though winter withholds

the mountain stood still
daring a mouse who presumed
the two were equals

ants in peonies
ambling through the deep petals
a kind of Eden

the steady light rains
soothe, pacify and console
cleanse my spirit

                        autumn lies subdued
                        from out of the noonday sun
                        its last butterfly

a streak of yellow
comes right down the darkened sky
a finch by surprise

                        in your great city
                        you never heard it before
                        listen, a bird calls

as a startled fawn
flees into the deep forest
day fades into night

twelve angriest crows
pursuing a great horned owl
exhausted to death

the fires of nature
needing to survive this way
a forest's new growth

a meteor streaks,
before two worlds can collide
my dream must now end

eagles on treetops
swaying in the mighty wind
such perfect command

the firefly ascends
a star its hoped for playmate
the grasses again

the still perfect day
sun and flower, moon and tide
twilight lingering

when sighting a star
quickly through the universe
that strange view of time

a mat of gold grass
softly cushions the meadow
for wandering boys

                              what gentle brook flows
                              that is not nature's own shrine
                              a whispering there

circus animals
about in a brick jungle
this far harsher place

                              the six inch rattler
                              keeps striking at my thick boot
                              teaching to defend

first we did not know
the birds are playing a great game
these wiles of nature

spring's great ascendance
begins so slowly, softly
caterpillar hairs

from old winter's bag
teasing on this tenth of March
with a summer day

such large mosquitoes
draining more blood from our arms
the boys' strangest game

so strong the weed roots
holding tight to mother earth
her dandelions

rivers wind to seas
seas congregate in oceans
how many raindrops

a circling hawk
so high above the broad field
its thousand glances

all winter's sharpness
tapering here to the point
of an icicle

swallows suppering
on the last remaining streak
of diminished day

the wild raspberries
suddenly in that thick brush
treasuring childhood

most generously
the clouds and trees and daisies
sharing in the winds

a throng of Adams
descending on the orchard
forbidden fruit gorged

from moose to chipmunk
always nature's great surprise
from snake to possum

the scent of old men
on a slightest hint of breeze,
three deer vanishing

to once discover
something so very precious
as baby rabbits

on this foggy night
we have become the ocean
tidal wave of dew

who would have the moon
must first speak its language
and flatter it so

blinding snow and gale
I struggle through the deep drifts
just then a lost world

sunbeams on flowers
how softly candlelight glows
on the smiles of saints

the bees miles apart
red rose and chrysanthemum
twilight's sweet mingling

a thousand bobbing
white lilies of the valley
summer giddiness

in winter's deadness
all of nature quite content
still, silent, alone

a child's sand castle
that moment of youthfulness
in life's sweeping tide

now well past midnight
grunion wriggling on the beach
the moon's silver spawn

walking through farm fields
such exhaustion it brings
each furrow a hill

from the far North woods
its fresh winds rush to my door
exhaling pine breaths

I had just noticed
all the crickets strange silence
then this first raindrop

sparrows still chirping
all the stalks in my garden
a fine winter place

inside the chapel
hear the rustle of tall corn
whispered thanksgivings

the children press near
one of them gently touches
the stricken young bird

the moon breaking through
from a stormy dark midnight
somewhere peace on earth

fleeing roadrunner
but you never fly away
poking fun instead

rolling tumbleweeds
still along the great highways
bringing back the past

Indian summer
even the year would tarry
in autumn's waning

through skeleton groves
the autumn breezes reach out
pulling shawls tighter

summer so profuse
it perfumes the night as well
oh generous world

through the smoke and mist
blend the colors of autumn
into pumpkin orange

miraculous rose
such are heaven's fragrances
the beloved saint

a black widow spider
I study it carefully
attuned to all life

trusting ladybug
tucking your delicate wings
the palm of my hand

what remains of night
but lovers and the lonely
crickets too would sleep

a snail's slow struggle
only children imagine
the moon on its back

euphorically
above that roar of the surf
gulls or sailors' ghosts

weary traveler
gently like snowflakes and mists
a kind word to you

in spring's alertness
now as then the same youthful cries
beckon summer come

the summer sand box
a child-master painting there
with elegant strokes

the clouds are shaping
into anything at all
these dreams of summer

the countless cacti
what purpose so idly by
ah, lovely desert

these skeletal fins
deep canyon walls red glowing
fighting the deluge

to walk through the clouds
a great mountain's many worlds
it is not snowing

summer suns, picnics
generations passing by
the willow weeping

a bird on the wing
snatches a climbing spider
this web of our world

beseeching someone
do the winds but call the pines
we who should listen

the largest apple
espied from a lowly limb
the risks of our lives

two hundred blackbirds
in most precise maneuvers
their cloak of darkness

it paints all nature
as it sculpts the fine summer
a sun's godliness

a farmhouse appears
look it is a small village
that magic of mists

the role of crickets
a nocturnal calling forth
their song is our dream

the crash of the surf
seagulls and sandpipers too
we hear its great call

one by one those lights
of the universe are lit
throughout a tall pine

all the warm white snows
of January blossoms
veiling the orchard

golds, greens and scarlets
the geese remain high above
a land all afire

from summer's excess
a fly darts into my eye
this likely meeting

white clouds stretching far
warm then cool then warm again
a hide and seek sun

thoughts drifting with dusk
into the waves of dark hills
eons come in view

                              beavers build their dam
                              ants drag a large grasshopper
                              all spring in earnest

the cry of a hawk
lends nature its own true voice
fills the Grand Canyon

                              I stared at the deer
                              five seconds our world stood still
                              then its parting leaps

walking a woodland
in countless pristine places
the self would vanish

subjects of cities
will never know all they lost
along a wooded way

slight breeze, faint moonlight
and fruit flies find the orchard
midnight ecstasies

from somewhere out there
in the darkness and terror
a white owl swoops down

the seeds of milkweed
float lightly on summer's breath
children jump for joy

outlined that high hill
a tree becomes the great sketch
of all the cosmos

orange and black orioles
safely hide their rare beauty
wary of our world

enthralled by insects
a small walleye surfaces
firm the eagle's grip

its great beak tells all
the insistent whippoorwill
sings, dines the forest

the shape of a rose
then that color and fragrance
all June's perfection

ants swarming the earth
in and out every crevice
what be their great task

always that same song
birds never tire telling us
of all the glory

leaves flitting about
zigzag, up down, yellow blur
each fall's butterfly

here the morning star
reflected in a dewdrop
this oneness of life

from the rippling stream
a bright speck of flower gold
pan filled with my dreams

that stranger passing
if I knew him well enough
likely my best friend

the desert's deep breaths
then winds through mountain passes
pulled by the far sea

                              the birdseed lady
                              to be loved so by pigeons
                              this bitter cold day

nobody listens
to hear the sparrow singing
only its heart tells

                              warm breeze and cold gusts
                              whirlwind on a Kansas plain
                              all nature's outrage

the harvest over
only tatters in the wind
a scarecrow dying

white blossoms falling
mix with the last snow flurry
robins hesitate

the sturdy forest
all it has built of our world
all it must still do

steep the granite cliff
nature's own great monuments
high the redwood spire

the gentle raindrops
become pools, streams and rivers
rushing to the sea

a Western ghost town
abandoned but threatening
moth caught in a web

stifling August day
the quiet desert town sleeps
itself a mirage

drag the old canoe
from the river back to the lake
youth's grand adventure

those loud swift raindrops
and maybe the lightning too
pursuing me home

wood-burning winters
with the aroma this night
our forest city

snow, rain, rose and leaf
amidst all the upheaval
each season's softness

birds with bears at play
nature's great equalizer
the slight feathered wing

a butterfly feasts
the child slowly reaches out
to gently hold wings

                              marlins gathering
                              swirl high in their great signal
                              come a dozen more

that hardy old oak
baked in all the suns that shined
froze in all the snows

                              partridges erupt
                              from beneath the startled boy
                              no hunter at all

the horse's old torn hat
it is not the least funny
dumb, exhausted beast

for the child and old man
the view is never the same
nor spring and autumn

a pigeon feather
floating down the sky of bricks
fills a beggars cup

motionless waters
a slightest tug on my line
deep, deep the big fish

in gentlest fog
the dew that softly gathered
weighs upon clover

long the glacier came
through gentle hills and moraines
this lake of one's own

their nest had broken
now only the beaks of crows
would end such hunger

the few barn swallows
lovers of rain on wood roofs
let them, let us be

to kill a firefly,
the child had even wondered
would the stars go out

                              a once careless owl
                              and faintest glimpse of the sun
                              goes hungry tonight

these bits of pollen
over miles of gusty winds
to my runny nose

                              twenty foot dead drop
                              eerie squeal of a wood rat
                              hawk rising, rising

intent on nectar
but does the bee consider
that far thunderhead

from sand to starlight
the vast desert beckons me
a lizard springs free

the butterfly's path
joy its every movement
endless frolicking

a colorless sea
but oh, the sky sharing now
its abundant blue

staring and dozing
all day those dotted puddles
counterpoints to thought

who is the maestro
conducting these woodland suites
my seat an old log

swallows zigzag flight
we are dizzy from watching,
summer silliness

these wild blackberries
a most sumptuous of feasts
set the fairies' table

could I imagine
crows awkwardly munch the field
a song from their breasts

springtime arriving
just now this warmth of the sun
robins there at rest

at shadows' ending
somewhere in a sliding sea
the day disappears

forest primeval,
shattered songs and stillnesses
a war's sacrilege

glorious sunrise
nightingales should be singing
flowers bursting forth

                    primordial dread
                    agile, sleek, smooth, wondrous snake
                    respecting it so

twilight from the pier
bugs as enthused about me
as I the sunset

                    that tastiest treat
                    a carrot fresh from the ground
                    the boy's own garden

ducks on an ice pond
all night that perilous cold
nature's bosom there

in midnight stillness
the same owl rests on my ledge
what would it tell me

a child is asking
will summer last forever
first catch the firefly

trees rustling of thirst
roots strain in their deep seeking
drought paining the earth

what do you see there
looking intently the sky
what do I not see

a new wilderness
from barren rock teeming life
how resourceful she

the shade of maples
chickens on the farmhouse lawn
shaping a memory

all these falling leaves
each autumn its great ending
such is the sadness

fooling all nature
a squirrel climbs its tall tree
nesting with the birds

gleaming grain of sand
deeper and deeper visions
the fathomless skies

if keenly observed
in the face of one flower
all nature's glory

adventurous bees
that distant, rich countryside
its bounty homebound

a butterfly rests
on the back of a huge sow
summer harmonies

this hope of all spring
four brown eggs of a ruffed grouse
gently lies the hen

a lizard appears
back and forth between two worlds
then it vanishes

drinking from puddles
the bird with a broken wing,
these binds of our lives

one with nature now,
in the river's reflection
myself a stranger

great Andromeda
in your faintest of starlight
the faith that is mine

the simple insect
of nature's revelation
wondrously it climbs

the tide sweeping in
a great ocean comes to me
my day's journey ends

another autumn
disappears in veils of mist
all who are gone now

poor unknowing birds
though there be an instinct too
that sings God's praises

the farmer watches,
in a patch of red clover
his bull resting now

gathering vultures
seem to mock the graceful deer
limping to its death

whispering faintly
a light rain speaks to the pond
and all understand

by the old cafe
a few less plump pigeons
dare I imagine

decrepit beggar
his pitiful ode to spring
pleading for a dime

the child plants a seed
then dreams of his apple tree
that long sleep of youth

an old man listens
the ticking grandfather clock
and distant thunder

on a country road
we must stop and honk and shout
horses running off

the drake and its mate
a hunter raises his gun
but only silence

a hound sniffs the ground
midst so many slightest scents
knowingly plods on

in nature's harsh place
six mice burst upon our world
wails the newborn spring

along Milky Way
the stars as many as sands
what purpose at all

sixty-beat seconds
the wings of a hummingbird
and my spirit soars

the rains keep coming,
in that world of an insect
a leaf is an ark

a thoroughbred runs
with that grace of lineage
wild steed in its heart

the bee is groggy
drunk on all of summertime
its great task finished

in winter's ending
its massiveness lingers on
the still-frosted pane

one lark the vast skies
all of life has come to this
autumn's final song

those marvelous friends
but now the vanished city
how bleak November

a bluebird rising
then itself becomes the sky
in summer's fancy

lion of the lake
a muskie leaps for the sun
such a will to live

mystery of time
still mighty Colorado
keeper of all dreams

it takes a fine soul
to see the end of our lives
in a fallen wren

in all night's fullness
that choir of the universe
so silently sings

rarest butterfly
but what to do this moment
caught, in my haiku

not a soul in sight
and nature the one great foe
ah, happy golfer

bare, brown maple tree
but that nun in the window
not the slightest sad

the carousel stops
its music fading away
a childhood ending

those whispering leaves
the woods are a scary place
and secrets abound

this Hawaiian calm
peeking in the volcano
a giant asleep

the tide sweeping in
such a marvel that moonbeam
its magical touch

has someone asked this,
that perfect hue of blue sky
of all the colors

nature's peacefulness
would that it could heal all hearts
a swan glides by me

bonfires burning low
in autumn's shadowy mix
joy turns to sadness

before the warm hearth
fine old tales and memories
there in dancing flames

on a craggy ridge
blending with the Western sky
bighorns glide as clouds

this longest June day
will we now see the elves,
how brief was that dream

lonely railroad tracks
telling of some distant place
hobo of my heart

the sun long gone now
but the moon holding its light
then magnolias

the gentle river
took half a haiku away
summer sleepiness

three hundred species
their mountain sanctuary,
we birders devout

that stolen flower
brought an eternal summer
childhood memory

a garden pathway
will the old couple recall
another springtime

those high granite cliffs,
who carved such elegant forms
the eons were here

a balloon rising
the sad child can only stare
and think of heaven

rolling waves of wheat
this fondness of soft breezes
strolling golden lane

a lame-leg rabbit
now overcoming its fear
the children staring

with enough knowledge
all could live in some forest
the fearsome toadstool

only the wild bee
knows how to extract its gold
the flowers mating

the years disappear
she is his young love again
a moonlight's faint glow

not the least aloof
a peacock struts in the park
its creatureliness

long days in the field
what farmer does not confide
his faithful scarecrow

behind nature's veil
a mouse cannot see the hawk
its circle shrinking

all those many loves
carved into the huge tree trunk
the oak still standing

the diamond sands
so is its precious appeal
this beautiful beach

a desert deluge
cacti craving the flashflood
a rat has its fill

observe thc May fly
see if caring how to spend
its one day of life

many beads of stars
might I have prayed them all
only morning came

a daddy longlegs
we play with it fearlessly
by that name only

          oh butterfly born
          of sunbeam and morning dew
          I name thee "springtime"

the thrust of pine shoots
through that deep rock of winter
to the moon and stars

          ants much too busy
          to take notice of giants
          now all about them

gone the buffalo
but their image charges on
in granite and cloud

coming and going,
at nightfall whole herds of deer
sharing a salt lick

slowly the spider
with its slight bit of poison
sets out the fast fly

a mockingbird sings
in the perfectly still night,
lyrics of moonlight

the long night howls on
so distinctly of treetops
and blackened chimneys

an old falconer
lusts as a beast for the kill
then that deadly dive

winter's hopeful hours
and watching the bird feeder
for some rarer kind

once a month cigar
a half foot of fertile field
breathed into the soul

on these chill evenings
flowers troubled by the frost
still, the sad beauty

ah, a visitor
overnight the bits of cork
hungry, fumbling mouse

these abandoned shafts
what cave-ins and miners' cries,
not one step closer

swing to the pale moon
in summer's euphoria,
hope corn on the cob

December creampuffs
only it is snow that drifts
the children tasting

skipping over them
a boy tries to spare the ants
but the rain will come

we change so slowly
when had I grown this older
day turning twilight

the girls jumping rope
all of spring's excitedness
their dancing shadows

a buzzing, buzzing
one concern in all the world
this flea in my ear

the startled goldfish
as a cunning raccoon strikes
by streaks of lightning

taps a woodpecker
the beat of red, white and black
that sound of hunger

her lemonade stand
a child's first feeble venture
in so strange a world

from his father's arms
a 2-year old points the far light
flicker of a star

season to season
wandering, wondering on
haiku to haiku

summer only comes
with the call of countless birds
and one child's longing

the old haunted house
high on a hill darkly broods
warning all children

he lifts the cardboard
as if frightened by tigers,
the scampering mice

laden with raindrops
to this one little flower
the vast skies have come

all spring awakens
as the warm sun arouses
one bud its slumber

the gold of maples
coloring these many moods
of autumn's richness

soon the bird will fly
having spent itself in song
to die gracefully

bent over flowers
the deer becomes statue-like
a garden figure

hibernating bear
one pulse beat more, one dream's worth
at last of springtime

my parents' gravesite
in a gentle summer breeze
all eternity

first rays of sunrise
and a new golden haiku
on each flower's face

in an apple tree
suddenly summer appears
fleet Wisconsin spring

let winter come now
moonlight on glistening snow
such peace and quiet

across the orchard
on a thousand white petals
the bird's faint shadow

in the winds of spring
midst soaring birds, racing clouds
he runs with his kite

by the trembling pines
one moment of awareness,
I must not forget

all the bird's redness
fills a whole white wintry field
my fullness of heart

sultry Sonora
we become the sun itself
ravished by its rays

is it the skylark
lifts the dawn lowers the dusk,
all life's mystery

sight and sense recall
that very moment of youth
apple blossom time

tracking a lone fawn
that ventured out to taste leaves
the cool of evening

just beyond mid March
I hear the great wakening
one bird calling out

a fir tree's fullness,
dwelling on all that beauty
I am wiser now

all nature's wonder,
what merest of accidents
and mindless world

blue beak and gold winged
your forever silent song
bird of paradise *

as the moon rises
the days of Menomonee
darken forever **

* The Bird-of-paradise flower has a spectacularly exotic perennial bloom. It grows profusely in the Mediterranean-like climate of Southern California, and has been officially adopted by and identified with the city of Los Angeles. Honoring my adopted home and many friends there, I rewrite this Haiku as follows:

> blue beak and gold winged
> you are our city singing
> bird of paradise

** The 4-mile long Menomonee River Parkway in Wisconsin extends from Currie Park Golf Course to the Village of Wauwatosa along a pristine stretch of winding river. To the youth of the 1940s it was an idyllic place with bridle path, deep wooded sections, a gorgeous lagoon, varied wildlife (once we came upon a family of Mink), many broad grassy areas for football, baseball and picnicking, and a secluded "island" inhabited by the oldest Oak tree in the State. Hoyt Park swimming pool, the largest in the nation when built in 1939 as a C.C.C. project (6,000 swam there on hot summer days) is adjacent to the Parkway, as is Blue Mound Country Club site of the 1933 P.G.A. golf championship won by Gene Sarazen, and the 80-acre campus of an architecturally striking Mount Mary College. When a star with the Milwaukee Bucks N.B.A. basketball team, Kareem Abdul Jabbar had a home on the west side of the river a quarter mile north of the North Avenue Bridge, another project of the depression era. I lived a block from this park, and the romance of one's young life is perfectly captured by that marvelous world of our little retreat on the Menomonee River. There was one last time we played there as signified by this haiku of mine.

A Final Thought

"In nature's infinite book of secrecy a little I can read," wrote Shakespeare. One person's awareness of the natural world is meager indeed. However, if these simple sightings are relished, it is witness enough as the spirit is nourished this way and upon further reflection.

That whole expanse of primal glory has been carefully, affectionately set before us. Then surely such a realm hints of paradise, in some sense deliverance already ours in this pure appreciation of God's goodness and wonder.

May it be a kind of communion now. Perhaps there is a duty to observe that divine artistry from time to time; or, as readers and writers of Haiku, acknowledge his majesty in this one little corner of creation so enthusiastically identified.

> earth and sea and sky
> what love that grand dispersing
> the gift of our world   Heil

978-0-595-37471-7
0-595-37471-9

20686313R00124

Made in the USA
Lexington, KY
19 February 2013